PROMISED FRUIT

ALMA ROSA ALVAREZ
MICHELLE ST. ROMAIN WILSON

SINGING BIRD PRESS

Copyright 2020
by Alma Rosa Alvarez and
Michelle St. Romain Wilson

All rights reserved. No portion of this book may be reproduced or transmitted without written permission from the authors.

Cover photo: Michelle St. Romain Wilson

ISBN-10: 1645508706
ISBN-13: 9781645508700

singingbirdpress@gmail.com
Singing Bird Press
P.O. Box 3328
Ashland, OR 97520

For Mom, who always believed in my writing
*   --Michelle St. Romain Wilson*

For Vince and Patty Wixon who asked when, and Liora Katherine who said when. For John Anthony Almaguer and John Rafael Almaguer.
*   --Alma Rosa Alvarez*

Table of Contents

Introduction	1
The Imperative of Poetry	2
Berry Picking	4
Blue Jay	5
Consider the Crocus	6
The Turning	8
The Poet Sees His Grandmother's Face	11
Mummies	13
Louisiana Night	15
Nesting	18
Salvatore Ferragamo	20
Embodiment	22
Inconspicuous	25
Mari Lu	26
Marshalls' Worker	28
Isaac	31
What They Say	33
Amina	35
Bowl of Tangerines	37
As the World Waits for a (Possible) Nuclear War	39
Atonement	42
The Only Thing You Know	44
Dark Mother	46
Bodhicitta	48
Ancient Melody	51
Singing	53
To Live in the Time of Mangoes	56

Introduction

This collection of poems is an offering. We reflect on themes ranging from joys we experience as individuals to challenges we face as a world community. We write as women, mothers, and educators. Through the poetic lens we observe more deeply ordinary items so easily taken for granted, so that we can see them anew, in their wonder, their splendor. Often, the small details lead us to reflect on larger truths. Sometimes these truths startle us. Sometimes they sadden or anger us, particularly when what is revealed is a world that can be imperfect and unjust. We are convinced, however, that looking at our world with honesty and clarity gives us an opportunity to respond with love and compassion. We have enjoyed collaborating on this project, learning and growing from each other's words and perceptions. We hope you enjoy reading these poems.

Michelle St. Romain Wilson (MSW) and Alma Rosa Alvarez (ARA)

The Imperative of Poetry

Words save lives
the voice inside my head
repeats incessantly
(true to poetic form:
rhythm, repetition)

words strung together
neatly as small lights
are strung across
backyard fences
to light up the
dark night
bring wonder
and the promise
of (possible) sightings
of fairies to an
unsuspecting audience
words strung together
just so
light up the darkened
mind and the body
clenched with fear
or hopelessness

We can hang our hope
on this string of words
offered quietly or boldly
in times of dark night

knowing that –
remembering that –
invisible worlds
of sacred beings
live around and beside and
within us

Words strung together
that come from that place
remind us of this
and open bright lights of hope
within us

small lights of hope
and wisdom
and wonder

within us

      MSW

Berry Picking

People's body parts
pop out
of bushes
while young lovers
look on:

here,
an ample behind
made rounder
by patterned flowers
there,
bare, white arms
as if embracing
here,
a head covered
by a weathered straw hat--

the smell of berries
sweating
the evening air

                    ARA

Blue Jay

Despite your black bridle
and perky crest
I had disliked you
for being the bully
of the feeders
for sometimes
being bold enough
to consume others' eggs
or nestlings.

Master mimic
of gardens and fields
I misjudged
how your voracious appetite
which in human terms
translates to gluttony and hoarding
turns   through forgetfulness
into   seed   dispersal
              a replenishing of the ecosystem

I misjudged
how your actions
render wasps' carefully gathered fibers
from dead wood
and plant stems
empty   and uninhabitable.

                      ARA

Consider the Crocus

I have seen the way
the crocus, hesitant and slight,
pokes its tiny petals
above the frozen ground

almost beyond belief
that something
so beautiful and bright
can appear in this
barest time of year

With precision to the calendar –
February – the cold, white month
of short, icy days
the crocus rises from a
winter sleep

and though it is easy to
stomp it back into the
frozen Earth
even without thinking
only from lack of practice
in the dark, frozen months
of caring for something
so delicate and beautiful

though it would be easy
to trample it without noticing

each time I see these tiny golden petals
I halt, stunned by this simple act
of flower pushing again to the sun
(though it cannot see it through
winter clouds)

Stunned into silence
as I remember, again,
the flower must reach to the sky
and I, I must bow
to its body-wisdom
and reach again to the light
I cannot see
the light I do not always believe in
but which pulls me
hesitant, tiny, tender

beyond this frozen ground
beyond belief
surrendering to a body-wisdom
as ancient
as this Earth

Surrendering
to the light
I cannot see

                    MSW

The Turning

I turn the Earth in our garden
my fingers crusted with winter soil
black, inky layers on top
moist mud beneath
I start close to the fence
tugging at roots of weeds taking over
pulling from the soil
layers of dead leaves
and tiny bits of last year's harvest
we did not eat:
dying pea shoots, the artichoke that
did not bloom to fullness

I move to the herbs and as I turn
and till the Earth
the smells rise to meet me
before my mind names each plant:
spearmint, green onions, cilantro

I give myself to the garden in this moment
unearthing all that died in winter
mirroring all that dies in me
hastily pulling debris aside
hungrily digging deeper
waiting for more smells
wet Earth, rosemary, thyme, black mud

I dig as an archaeologist
might turn an ancient site
though not as gentle
and for no audience but myself

The garden will feed us
again this year
of this I am certain:
kale, lettuce, celery, zucchini, tomato

but first I must prepare it
first I must excavate
clearing layers of dead winter
as the soil opens before me

This is holy work
and I remember again
this mid-March afternoon
that all I've hoped for
is always here in this small patch
of garden outside the windows

through the dark winter nights
though we knew nothing about it
the earthworms were digging
making room for sprouting strawberries
to feed our hungers
in summer's heat

No matter what I believe
the Earth keeps turning
and seeds that fell last year
are sprouting now
no matter what I believe
carrots, celery, bok choy
come alive

I dig deeper and
the dirt beneath my fingernails
tells the story:
hope and death lie side by side
in my garden

I breathe the smells
in deeply
mingled now
seducing me

I give myself fully
to this ancient, constant
turning

                MSW

The Poet Sees His Grandmother's Face

My friend, Lawson,
a poet,
has not liked
computers.
He says that his poems
when they first arrive
come longhand.
Eventually
they make it
to the typewriter
where in writing them
he taps out a rhythm
but this isn't
what he likes
about typing.
What he likes
is how upon seeing
the words come up,
the typewriter
provides
a sufficient pause
to think   or to whiteout.

Recently, Lawson
has discovered
the internet—
repository of facts
and a connection
to a story he knew
from a different angle
the story of a grandmother
sitting on the porch
of a home,
recovered after Internment.

What a surprise,
to see her face,
and it made
the seventy-something year old man
transform
into the child
he was back then
and wonder
where he was
in relation to his grandmother.

His own parents
without a home
after camp
went to her place
and so the poet surmises
yes, there,
I must have been there
to the side of my grandmother
just outside
the scope of the lens.

And he smiles
to see her face
and at the knowledge
that through her
he knows his place.

ARA

Mummies

We insisted
we needed
to visit the mummies.

How could we not?
Star-attraction
of Guanajuato
that spun-off
a movie
where Mexican wrestlers
fought them?

My father is hesitant,
finding the idea
of seeing anonymous bodies
profane.
We expect him to be relieved
when we encounter the first mummy
clothed,
with a history
a name.

As we move
further in
it is undeniable--
there *is* something hideous
and I wonder
if morticians
now-a-days,
sew our mouths shut
when we die.

The worst are the rooms
filled with babies,
dead
days after
their entry
in this world,
some still clothed
in saint outfits
a testament
to innocence and purity.

After one room
we hang back
in a narrow hall
while my mother,
who is afraid of horror movies
who cannot stand
the sight of blood
who gags
when she smells
others' shit
is enthralled
with the cuteness
of a little mummy's shoe
and another little mummy's foot.

ARA

Louisiana Night

My father's family spoke French
in a dialect only we
could understand
and still so much lingers
like music playing gently
in deep crevices of my mind

Memories of voices trailing
down the hall
after we, the children,
went to bed:
mais oui, mon cheri –
lyrical words moving together
sliding through the warm, thick
summer nights
as daddy longlegs dangled
from my ceiling and
puppies slept, snoring gently
as though not to wake me
though I did not
could not
sleep

Belly full of gumbo
hot and spicy
sweet taste of gulf shrimp
and silky okra
warming me
still

Still
I cannot sleep

Memories of climbing
our large oak tree
branches reaching out
over the house
protecting us from thunder
and lightning
and threats of hurricane winds:
only warm, healing rain
showers us now
lulling me into
the secrets of the night

Stars come out
one by one by one
shyly first
then piercing
through the darkness

Quietly now
voices dim
belly full
I drift into
a sleepy sleep
arms and legs resting still
in my dreams
against our old
and beautiful
guardian oak tree

quiet now
quiet

Storms are passing now
and the daddy longlegs
has finally disappeared
no longer hanging from my ceiling
at last
at last

I sleep

                        MSW

Nesting

My sister has complained
time and time again
about the disorder
of pots and pans
in my deep caverned cabinets

I work hard
to organize the space
imposing   Order
imposing   Logic
through the hard, metal shelves
that will
compartmentalize
our culinary habits

I remember doing this before
but with different areas
of our lives
like the linens
our clothes
our shoes
all in preparation
for your coming

Now, two weeks before you leave,
I am—methodical
I am—motivated.
You break my concentration
         tentatively
when you call me over
to see
how outside your window
the mourning dove
is on the ledge of the bird feeder.

This bird, that gives me so much joy,
builds flimsy platform nests of twigs
that fall apart
in storms.

                ARA

Salvatore Ferragamo

My son
with saved up
allowance money
from easy chores
and indulgent grandparents
tries on
Salvatore
Ferragamo
shoes.

Salvatore Ferragamo
who first dabbled
in shoe design
to provide
his sister
with First Communion shoes
wrote how his shoes
made "the foot act
like an inverted pendulum."

My son decides
on cap-toe oxford shoes
that cost
more than half
of our vacation money

Salvatore Ferragamo's legacy
goes three generations back.
Two generations back
from my son
there were two girls
working their father's fields

for the promise of cloth
or in the year of a good yield
money for the dressmaker
to have dresses
ready for display
for the town's fiesta.

                ARA

Embodiment

I hate him, he said
speaking of the terrible god of war
who took down the world
before our eyes
as we chewed on popcorn
in a darkened movie theater

How could anyone be like that?
I hate him,
the second time saying it
to emphasize his certainty

Hatred hurts the one holding it,
I say
and though he may not understand
he does not dispute my claim

How can anyone be like that?
I wonder
though I do not say it
how can evil exist
hatred take hold in hardened hearts
until the only answer
seems to be destruction
creating a terrible, darkened balance
lives taken and given
by the blind eye
of dictator rule

Easy, I say
to his words of hate:
drop by drop
your hatred and mine
and that of others
we do not know
collects into a cauldron
we cannot control
until, pushed by pressure
from invisible collective pain
turned to stone
someone will arise
embodying that which we
push down
embodying every dark
thought and pain
and stony wall
erected within us

we create this dark theater
within ourselves
and play it out
on a stage larger
than we can understand
or control

drop by drop
thought by thought

Easy, now,
easy
whichever direction
this story will go

this is where
it all begins

      MSW

Inconspicuous

You
are over
six feet tall
and your beard
and trek
from Midwest
flatlands
to the Great Pacific Northwest
makes you look
like a rugged, mountain man
but we know better—
we saw
inconspicuous
in the evergreen
of your Christmas tree
an ornament
of handblown glass
a pear
lovely
in its clearness and simplicity
and precious
for its fragility.

      ARA

Mari Lu

You are some wacked out
kind of wonderful
Mari Lu
I first saw you strut
your skinny ass
to church
sweaty and out of breath
from the twenty mile
bike ride
which you claim
was worth
the price of admission
for saving your soul
and it was even more worth it
because you were desperate—
and we could sense it
despite a cosmopolitan veneer
acquired in Barcelona
which made you
keep most things
close to your vest

But in Wal-Mart
you are friendly
cashiering, making chit-chat
and the customers
they all like you
calling you
Hey, Mari Lu
which in Medford, Oregon
sounds like Hey Mary Lou
and you return
the familiarity

calling them hon
giving design tips
because they've given you
really, without thinking
a glimpse
into their lives
and for a minute I think
we've misjudged you
until you part
from the client before you
with a laugh
whose underbelly
is crazy and desperate.

                      ARA

Marshalls' Worker

Every day
the woman
with sensible shoes
stocks
prices
and displays
shoes
that are a season
behind
or shoes
that are in season
but are
the miscellany
of fashionable
department
stores
and everyday
she serves
up advice
solicited
by other workers
and clients alike.

One day
it's to a young
black lesbian
desperate
because her girlfriend
has broken up
with her.
The woman
who was once homophobic
suggests what she knows:

flowers and candy
and saying
I'm sorry.

Another day
it's to a client
with bleach blonde hair
and tight J Lo jeans
who on her weekly visit
confides about her fiancé's family:
how they hate her
for cradle robbing
their tender boy
who upon marrying her
will not only become
a husband
but a father
to her three children.
She tells her
to hold her temper
but not let anyone
trample her.

One day
it's listening
to another worker
the man with the tattered shoes
who daily
eats the same
watery soup
but dignifies it
with a napkin
on his lap
while he worries
about his twin children
whom he will never see
grow up

because he'll die
in a hit
and run,
sometime
later on.

The Marshalls' worker
keeps busy
in what she mostly thinks
are insignificant chores
and comes home tired.

                        ARA

Isaac

The homeless man
who antagonized
a worker
at the local fast food joint
for being gay
finally got his ass
thrown in the can
when he wielded
a machete
at your friend
and you
in an act of love
put your hand
in the way.

The machete has created
another life line
on your palm.
Maybe this groove
will give you better luck
will help you forget
the mother
who in tooting the rock
pimped her children out
some not yet
in grade school.

Maybe this life line
will help you forget
that to deal with your pain
you've developed
your own addictions
that have you ambling
through the streets

in a fierce survival stance
that doesn't represent
the real you—
a person who takes on
the burdens of the world.

                    ARA

What They Say

What they say
Freddie Gray
is how
a picked-up
preacher man
riding along
in the police van
heard you
hurling yourself
inside
banging
the reinforced
metal of the walls,
no matter
that you
were restrained
by leg irons
and hand cuffs,
a sack of stuff
with no seatbelt on
as the van sped away
to learn you
to behave
and not look a cop
directly in the face.
The blame
keeps coming back
to you again
so many arrests:
a thief
a guy caught with Mary Jane.
It's like the time
Your papa sued
for the brain-damage
you and your sisters sustained

for exposure
to lead paint
and the landlord
blamed
your mama and crack

but I don't
blame you
and I don't
believe them.

                        ARA

Amina

1.
After you
and the other girls
went missing
all that we had left
was an aerial photo
of your burned out school

How were you
a smart, privileged girl
to know?
It was the dead of night
and at the time
your worst nightmare
was sitting exams
but it would become
      abduction
it would become
      violence
it would become
      trafficking
it would become
      mothering

2.
Amina
you have been found—
wandering,
wandering
near the Sambisa Forest
and you tell us
how some of the girls
have died

but how most
have survived
the depths
where the density
of thorny bushes
and rubber
black plum
and tamarind trees
have conspired
with the enemy
to keep them captive.

Now
your hopes
are to be reunited
with your mother
who has survived
your absence
and the passing of your father
You are hoping
that escaping
will be worth it—
that the community
will not be hostile
or shun you
for bearing
a militant's child.

ARA

Bowl of Tangerines

How many children could that feed?
small white bowl of tangerines
one two three four five six
I count six
and see glimpses of a few more
hiding underneath

How many children could that feed?
at my house –
pantry stocked with nut bars and cookies
Ritz crackers and dried cranberries
and the refrigerator full
of cheese sticks
and mangoes
and homemade blackberry jam
at my house
that bowl would feed
three hungry teens
a tidy, happy snack
eaten almost without noticing
as they play cards
and laugh about the latest memes
and casually leave the last few sections
sitting uneaten on the table
when the doorbell rings
and the neighbor comes inside

How many children would that feed?
I am thinking now
(though I try not to)

of the ones held
inside wired fences in Texas
and Arizona
and New Mexico
the ones whose mothers walked them
a thousand miles or more
with hope and hunger
toward this land of plenty

how many of those children
would this bowl feed?

one two three four five six
I cannot stop counting
seven eight nine ten
too many to count
and we bicker amongst ourselves
whether or not to count them
among our own

How hungry we are
in this land of plenty

How empty we seem in this moment

                MSW

As the World Waits for a (Possible) Nuclear War

The alarm sings quietly
hesitant at first
and my hand reaches over
before eyes are open
to silence the sounds
of mechanical birds
I roll back onto the pillow
slowly opening my eyes
knowing I must
awaken

In the kitchen our tall teenager
pulls his sausage biscuit from
the microwave
sidestepping the cat
asking for breakfast

I pull a handful of
dry cat food from the
tupperware box
dropping it into the bowl
pet the cat
and whisper quietly,
good morning

Thirty minutes later
the middle school pair of children
move through the kitchen
spreading peanut butter on toast
stirring scrambled eggs in the pan

I pour coffee and listen
to their talk of math problems
and the definition of social justice
as they prepare for
an essay due next week

The newspaper sits on the coffee table
in the yellow plastic sleeve
still wet from morning rain
protected from water drops falling
from a clouded sky

I do not open it
not yet ready to see
stark headlines of chemical attacks
on children like ours
in far-away Syria
as far away from our kitchen scene
as Agrabar in Aladdin
or the mythical world of Narnia
where children don woolen coats
to protect themselves
from unbidden winter spread
over the world
by a fearful ruler

I do not want
to see if, in the dark of night,
our own country has sent warheads
to retaliate for children dying
at the hands of their own ruler
and, if so, how soon we may hear

about the promised strike
on us
as my children wrap
peanut butter sandwiches in saran wrap
and the cat purrs quietly on the couch
and I sip hot coffee
slowly

I look and see
we may be late for school today
and I wonder if I set the alarm
too late last night

Wonder if the alarm
went off
too late

                    MSW

Atonement

You are Grandpa George
not my grandpa
not even my kid's grandpa
but my kid's friend's grandpa

Something about you
reminds me
of Marco:
                the bloated face
                the affable style

You've made
the chore of being at a kid's party
less laborious.

Your hospitality
materializes
into beer
early
in the afternoon.

I accept
what I never accepted
or liked in Marco.

In Marco
drinking was disrespect
of my mother
a fight at my wedding
sloppy crying at a sad song.

You remind me of him,
Grandpa George,
and it's early afternoon,
yet drinking,
even
if it's encouraging a habit
seems redemptive.

      ARA

The Only Thing You Know

Go to the mat
and lie prostrate against
the cold winter within you

Go to the cathedral
eyes turned upward toward the light
streaming in through the glass mosaic
of Jesus tending sheep
knowing you will never feel his hand on you
as these sheep did long ago
and yet you stand
or kneel, hopeful,
for a different kind of touch
one that comes unbidden
melting muscles tight in your shoulders
muscles tight within your chest
heart beating slowly now
to the rhythm of your deepening breath

Go to the mountains
walking through pine trees
with your senses alert to some sign
that the spirits of the deep Earth
are listening
paying attention to the fall of humans
in the great cities and suburbs
hoping they will speak and tell you secrets
that you can tell your children
in the dark of night

when the wind swirls outside your window
and you doubt the rising
of the sun or
the coming of the Christ
though you never say this aloud

Go to the silence
for this is all you know to do
this is all the prophets and wise ones say to do

Go as if your life and
the lives of your children's children
depended on it

go to the mat
to still your beating heart
because it is the only thing
you know you can do

MSW

Dark Mother

Standing on this shore
  the energy of Ocean Mother
 moves through me
Send a gift, I ask
Suddenly at my feet a stone
 deep black, washed with white stripes,
 appears
I hold it in my palm where it fits
 as though carved into this hollow
Energy moves through me
 pulsing
I am the Dark Mother
 the stone speaks
I bring a message of surrendering
Be still and silent; allow waves of
 life and death
 to wash over you
Breathe
only breathe
Speak less; breathe more
Surrender to the waves and be swallowed
 whole
 by the vastness
Breathe in each wave unresisting
 and be carried
 beyond fear
 beyond words
 beyond thought

Breathe in each wave unresisting
 and find yourself
 part
 of the rhythm
Allow the wave to become you
 devour you whole
See, the wave carries you, releases you
 onto the shore you seek
With each breath you are carried deeper
 until at last
 your desire
 and the water
 are one
 washing you onto
 the shore
 your soul seeks
Surrender
Seek deeper
Surrender

     MSW

Bodhicitta

Start with the pain
the teacher of my body
and my mind that runs
to explain its cause:
surely
I have not cared for myself
well enough
surely
the fault line for this searing ache
is within my own psyche
surely
the fault
for this relentless ache
is my own

Dropping deeper
into the body of this pain
my greatest teacher
I burrow –
though I do not want to –
into the ache
in this human vessel
of my spirit

I know
more surely
that the pain is –
and is not –

my own
that the pain is reflected
from the larger bodies of life
all around me
bodies of life
that breathe me
into existence
each day

the faces of the
bodhisattvas of old
are carved from wood
and stone
carved to reflect
the light that
sears through all pain
each ache on the body
of this Earth

the face of the
bodhisattva
carved in wood
and stone
stands still
and silent
mouth closed
eyes open wide

taking in
each breath of suffering
breathing out
a larger light

taking in
each searing pain
slicing through it
like a sword

relentless
in the face
of suffering

relentless
in its light

shattering
piercing
the pain
that has no name

relentless
in this light

     MSW

Ancient Melody

I do not want to
hear the sounds of
engines running or
see the headlines of
the world on fire

I want to settle into the breath that moves
the sinews of my muscles
into a shape that soothes and holds
my weary psyche
allowing me
a moment to feel
that we are not alone
on this turning Earth
but held
by arms we cannot see
surrounded by
Ancient Ones
Who sing to us
breath by breath
reminding us
that we are not the first
and we are not the last
but the only ones
whose lives matter now
for we are the ones
who are here

We are the ones
who are here
and we are not alone

Sing to us
spirits of the Earth
and of the ancestors
please

sing to us

                MSW

Singing

Dying to be reborn
we are all seeds of light
    we must face our own darkness
    entering the womb of our Mother
    in this we become the empty space
    from which universes are born
Daily, hourly the deaths of our lives
remind us of the inevitable:
    dying to be reborn
    we enter the shadow and
    passing through into light
    we become something different
    than has ever been before
        Singing, singing
Entering unfamiliar landscapes
within and without
    inside, outside, turned around
    mirrors and clear glass
    smoky shadows we cannot tame
    or befriend, we must simply
    breathe through these moments of the death
Into shadow and light
spiraling through smoke which veils
    all markers we can read
    this very foreign land, ancient tongue
    speaks to us, haunting
    we hear
        Singing, singing
Language which the soul has never forgotten
begins to unravel itself in this maze of shadow

      as faintest sprays of light
      splatter themselves around, dancing
      on brilliant hues of purple, cobalt, aquamarine
      new landscape reveals itself
The mind must die to this beauty
disintegrating to the grace
      so that, much later, many, many moons later
      in shadow and light
      it may slowly reintegrate
      shadow now becoming light
The journey is long and dangerous and
perfectly safe in this bathtub
      ocean womb of the Mother
      the only predators are shadows
      mirrored of ourselves
      we must
            Sing, sing
New language slowly becomes decipherable
though the body is weak from the cycles
      of dying and birthing
      shedding and springing forth
      and the mind has finally gone blank
      seeking guidance from one who knows
      the terrain: the higher part of self
      in oneness with Divinity
We find this living in ourselves: Divinity
breathing us into being all along: Divinity
we must travel many moons of
shadow, light, until
            the lotus blossom
            springs into light

I am dying to be reborn
in each breath and day
      each year of this life
      dying into shadow
      birthing into light
Goddess
sing to me
      I am
            Singing, singing

                MSW

To Live in the Time of Mangoes

To live in the time of mangoes –
        of tree-ripened fruit falling
        splat
        at your feet
        a golden and red and orange-tinged gift
        from the Earth-Mother –
        this is what we wait for
        work for
        yearn to reach

I reach down and pick up the fruit
which has fallen like manna from the sky
holding this plump living food
in the palm of my hand
I understand – for a moment at least –
        that all promised fruit does blossom
        that here in the garden
        all hungers are fed
        that, indeed, we are all being led
        home again

For many months I have waited
for these mangoes to ripen and fall
I did not expect
they would taste so sweet
did not expect them to drop
at my feet with such splendor

even seeing the goodness growing before me
my mind trained to look for reasons to doubt
would not allow me to believe
that the fruit would taste good
would be given to me without my having to ask

This tree stands
as a Mother guardian
at the end of the driveway
watching over the house
and those of us who live here
with branches reaching out
over the gate
shading and blessing all who walk by
each day I come home to her, walk beneath her branches
each night I sleep within her protected space
dreaming dreams of new life
in childlike prayers, as I wait

For many months now I have waited
watching small buds of the Mother tree's fruit
grow into hard, green balls of promise
then slowly
       slowly
  lighten
    into red and orange
        and finally gold
  the sign of readiness
  the moment of birth
   and gift
at gold they drop --
       manna from the sky --

    and hardly recognizing the blessing
    of this gift
    I scoop them up
    thanking the Mother Tree

and go inside
where I hold this moment
in the palm of my hand
    all of life
    a blessing
    ripened fruit only waiting
    to be enjoyed

eating greedily
as a child full of hunger
I let the sweetness seep out on my face

living in this moment
of mangoes falling from the sky
in this moment
    if only a moment
I can dare to hope
filled with the sweetness
I can live
    and believe

May all hungers be fed
I hold each mango in my hands
    as a child
hold each mango as a prayer:
    may all of our hungers
    be fed

Here, at last, we come home:
    may our hungers
    be fed

                MSW

About the Authors

Michelle St. Romain Wilson has taught creative writing to children and teens through the Oregon Writing Project at Southern Oregon University (SOU) and the Academy program at SOU. She has a BA in English from Loyola University, New Orleans and an MA in English and Creative Writing from California State University, Sacramento. She loves living in the beautiful Rogue Valley with her wife, their three teenagers, and an assortment of pets.

Alma Rosa Alvarez is a professor of English at Southern Oregon University where she primarily teaches U.S. Ethnic Literature. She has a BA in English and Mexican-American Studies from California State University, Dominguez Hills. She has an MA and Ph.D. in English from University of California, Santa Barbara. Her favorite poets are Lucille Clifton and Gwendolyn Brooks, but she also has a special place in her heart for Pablo Neruda's odes.